Lucy's Garden

Mum bought two boxes of plants
for the flower garden.

"There are 60 plants altogether
in these boxes," said Lucy
as she counted them.
"30 are red and 30 are blue.
We could put blue ones
at each end of the garden,
and the red ones could go
in the middle."

"That's a good idea," said Mum.

"We will only need
a few plants to start with,
because this end of the garden
isn't very wide," said Mum.
"I will put **two** blue plants here,
and then I will put **two** more
under them."

"**Two** and **two** make **four**," said Lucy.

$$2 + 2 = 4$$

Now it was Lucy's turn.
"The garden is a bit wider now,"
she said.
"I will put **two** blue plants in here,
and I can fit **three** more under them.
That makes **five**.
Two and three make one more
than two and two."

$$2 + 3 = 5$$

How many blue plants
have they put in the garden altogether?

They have put nine blue plants
in the garden,
because **four** and **five** make **nine**.

Mum took **six** red plants from the box.
She put them in two groups of three.

$$3 + 3 = 6$$

Lucy took **seven** red plants,
because the garden was a bit wider.
She put **three** plants in one group,
and **four** plants in the other group.

$$3 + 4 = 7$$

Lucy and Mum were making
a number pattern with the plants.
What was it?

The number pattern was:

two and **two**   **two** and **three**
three and **three**   **three** and **four**

Mum took **eight** red plants from the box. She put them in two groups of four. "**Four** and **four** make **eight**," said Mum.

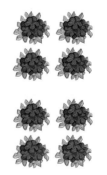

$$4 + 4 = 8$$

Lucy got **nine** red plants, because nine is one more than eight. She put them in two groups.

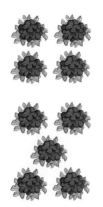

How many plants did Lucy put in each group?

Lucy put **four** plants in one group, and **five** plants in the other group.

4 + 5 = 9

Now all the red plants
were in the garden.

"This is the widest end of the garden,"
said Mum.
She took **ten** blue plants from the box,
and put them in two equal groups.

How many plants
did Mum put in each group?

Mum put five plants in each group, because **five** and **five** make **ten**.

$$5 + 5 = 10$$

Lucy counted the plants
that were left in the box.
There were 11.
"I can make the last pattern," she said.
"I will put **five** in the first group,
and **six** in the other group.
Then our garden will be finished."

5 + 6 = 11

1+1, 2+2, 3+3, 4+4, 5+5, 6+6
are all called **doubles**.

1+2, 2+3, 3+4, 4+5, 5+6, 6+7
are all called **near doubles**.

Doubles and near doubles

$1 + 1 = 2$
$1 + 2 = 3$

$2 + 2 = 4$
$2 + 3 = 5$

$3 + 3 = 6$
$3 + 4 = 7$

$4 + 4 = 8$
$4 + 5 = 9$

$5 + 5 = 10$
$5 + 6 = 11$

$6 + 6 = 12$
$6 + 7 = 13$

Top secret!

Doubles always name the **even** numbers: **0, 2, 4, 6, 8**.

Near doubles always name the **odd** numbers: **1, 3, 5, 7, 9**.